ID062942D

Carver

A LIFE IN POEMS

Carver

A LIFE IN POEMS

Marilyn Nelson

SCHOLASTIC INC.

New York   Toronto   London   Auckland   Sydney
Mexico City   New Delhi   Hong Kong   Buenos Aires

No part of this publication may be reproduced in whole or in part, or stored in a retrieval system, or transmitted in any form or by any means, electronic, mechanical, photocopying, recording, or otherwise, without written permission of the publisher. For information regarding permission, write to Front Street Books, Inc., P.O. Box 280, Arden, NC 28704.

ISBN 0-439-44339-3

Copyright © 2001 by Marilyn Nelson. All rights reserved.
Published by Scholastic Inc., 557 Broadway, New York, NY 10012, by arrangement with Front Street Books, Inc. SCHOLASTIC and associated logos are trademarks and/or registered trademarks of Scholastic Inc.

12 11 10 9 8 7 6 5 4 3 2 1   2 3 4 5 6 7/0

Printed in the U.S.A.   23

First Scholastic printing, September 2002

Designed by Helen Robinson

Again, and always: for Jake and Dora

I should appreciate it very much if the memory
of the great scientist George W. Carver would be
honored ...
— *Albert Einstein*

To let oneself seem inferior to what one is
is the supreme attribute of virtue.
— *Leo Tolstoy*

I thoroughly understand that there are scientists to
whom the world is merely the result of chemical forces
or material electrons. I do not belong to this class.
— *George Washington Carver*

A personal relationship with the Great Creator of all
things is the only foundation for the abundant life. The
farther we get away from self, the greater life will be.
— *George Washington Carver*

I will be with you in power.
— *George Washington Carver*

Carver

A LIFE IN POEMS

Out of "Slave's Ransom"

John Bentley, Diamond Grove, Missouri

There's a story to the name.
Had her since I was a colt myself.
Oh, I was a wild one,
up to my withers in oats, and
when Moses Carver comes to me
and begs me to go after
their slave-girl Mary and her son,
well, I never was one
to turn down good money.
Tracked the bushwhackers
two days south of here
and caught up with them
down in Arkansas: The girl,
already sold, had left them
holding a bundle of wet rags,
convulsive with fever and shook
by the whooping cough.
They were glad
to be shut of him.

When I handed him to Missus Carver,
you never seen such carrying-on.
All that over a puny black baby.
You'd have thought that Mary
was her sister or something.
Carver give me his best filly
as a reward.

Many's the winnings I've toasted
thanks to her and her colts.
This one's her fifteenth.
Look at the clean lines,
the sleekness, the self-respect.
His dam's a quarter Arabian,
and when you see him run you'll swear
he was sired by the wind.

c. 1864 Carver is born in Diamond Grove, Missouri. His mother, Mary, is a slave
owned by Moses and Susan Carver; Mary has an older son, Jim. Shortly
after George's birth, Mary and George are stolen; Moses Carver hires
John Bentley to find them. Bentley finds only the infant.

Prayer of the Ivory-Handled Knife

Susan Carver, 1871

Father, you have given us,
instead of our own children, your
and Mary's orphans, Jim and George.
What would you have us make
of them? What
kind of freedom
can we raise them to?
They will always be strangers
in this strange, hate-filled land.

Jim is a big help to Moses:
Thank you for their joined laughter
like morning mist over new-plowed fields.
And our little plant-doctor:
Now he's crushing leaves and berries
and painting sanded boards.
Thank you
for his profusion of roses
on our bedroom wall,
for his wildflower bouquet
in the sitting room,
his apples and pears beside the stove.

He ran out before breakfast,
saying he'd dreamed last night
of that pocket knife he's been
asking us and praying for.
A few minutes later he ran back up

from the garden, calling
Aunt Sue! Aunt Sue!
He'd found it in a watermelon,
ivory-handled,
exactly as he had dreamed.
Seemed like he all but flew
into my arms.
Oh, Father, gracious Lord:
How shall I thank you?

George and his brother, Jim (c. 1873). George (left) was frail and small
for his age. Jim was a few years older and strong and husky.

Watkins Laundry and Apothecary

Mariah Watkins, Neosho, Missouri

Imagine a child at your door,
offering to do your wash,
clean your house, cook,
to weed your kitchen garden
or paint you a bunch of flowers
in exchange for a meal.
A spindly ten-year-old, alone
and a stranger in town, here to go
to our school for colored children.
His high peep brought tears:
sleeping in a barn and all that,
nary mama nor kin,
but only white folks
he left with their blessing,
his earthly belongings
in a handkerchief tied to a stick.

I've brought a houseful of children
into this world, concentrating on
that needle's eye into eternity.
But ain't none of them children mine.
Well, of course I moved him on in.
He helped me with my washings,
brought me roots from the woods
that bleached them white folks' sheets
brighter than sunshine. He could fill
a canning jar with leaves and petals
so when you lifted the lid

a fine perfume flooded your senses.
White bodices and pantalettes danced
around George on my line.

He was sweet with the neighbor children.
Taught the girls to crochet.
Showed the boys
a seed he said held a worm
cupped hands warmed so it wriggled and set
the seed to twitching.
Gave them skills and wonders.
Knelt with me at bedtime.

He was the child the good Lord gave
and took away before I got more
than the twinkle of a glimpse
at the man he was going to be.
It happened one Saturday afternoon.
George was holding a black-eyed Susan,
talking about how the seed
this flower grew from
carried a message from a flower
that bloomed a million years ago,
and how this flower
would send the message on
to a flower that was going to bloom
in a million more years.
Praise Jesus, I'll never forget it.

He left to find a teacher that knew
more than he knew.
I give him my Bible.
I keep his letters
in the bureau, tied with a bow.
He always sends a dried flower.

Carver's school slate

1877 With the blessing of his foster parents, Moses and Susan Carver, George
moves to Neosho, about eight miles from Diamond Grove, to attend the
closest school for Negro children. This begins his long search for an education.

Drifter

Something says find out
why rain falls, what makes corn proud
and squash so humble, the questions
call like a train whistle so at fourteen,
fifteen, eighteen, nineteen still on half-fare,
over the receding landscapes the perceiving self
stares back from the darkening window.

George Washington Carver (c. 1879)

The Perceiving Self

Fort Scott, Kansas, 1879

The first except birds
who spoke to us, his voice high
and lilting as a meadowlark's,
with an undertone of windsong,
many-petaled as the meadow,
the music shaped and colored
by brown lips, white teeth, pink tongue.
Walking slowly, he talked to us,
touched our stamens,
pleasured us with pollen.
Then he squealed, a field mouse taken
without wingbeat,
with no shadow.
His yellow feet crushed past, running,
his bare legs bruised, he trampled, his spew
burned, his scalding urine.

The icedrift of silence.
Smoke from a torched deadman, barking laughter
from the cottonwoods at the creek.

1879 Carver witnesses a lynching, Fort Scott, Kansas.

Washboard Wizard

Highland, Kansas, 1885

All of us take our clothes to Carver.
He's a wizard with a washboard,
a genie of elbow grease and suds.
We'll take you over there next week;
by that time you'll be needing him.
He's a colored boy, a few years older
than we are, real smart. But he stays
in his place. They say
he was offered a scholarship
to the college. I don't know
what happened, but they say
that's why he's here in town.
Lives alone, in a little shack
filled with books
over in Poverty Row.
They say he reads them.
Dried plants, rocks, jars of colors.
A bubbling cauldron of laundry.
Pictures of flowers and landscapes.
They say he
painted them. They say
he was turned away when he got here,
because he's a nigger. I don't know about
all that. But he's the best
washwoman in town.

Old Settlers' Reunion

Ness County, Kansas

When I filed my claim back in April eighty-six,
this country weren't nothing but prairie grass,
rippling pink, blue, and yellow flowers
as far as the eye could squint.
Six years I cut tough turf from dawn
to way past suppertime, and drove my team back
to the sod house and barn
my first bride and I built together
like children playing with blocks.
Three of my children were born there.
I had two hundred acres, mostly in wheat.
To my north was Bothwick, to my south, Barnd.
To my east,
well, there's a story to tell.
Every other homesteader for counties around
had at least a wife, and most had families.
And all of us were white
except for the colored boy, George.
I think his name was Carver.

He kept to himself, pretty much,
but was always sort of joyous when you met, and humble,
like he'd just been told
the most marvelous, flattering joke.
He took in wash when he was more
hard up than usual, and played the accordion
so your feet didn't know where
your backside was going.

We never talked much. He lasted a couple of years,
then Lennon bought his hundred and sixty acres.
Sometimes, in the half-light of a winter's morning, I heard
George's clear tenor like a church bell over the snow.

1883 Carver attends high school in Minneapolis, Kansas. He adds a middle initial
to his name to distinguish himself from a man in town with the same name;
when asked what the "W." stands for, he jokingly answers, "Washington." He
joins the Presbyterian Church.
1884 He is rejected because of his race by Highland College, Highland, Kansas.
1886 He homesteads on the "sod house frontier" in Ness County, Kansas.

A Ship Without a Rudder

Helen Milholland, Winterset, Iowa, 1890

A new voice in church. I turned around to look.
A colored boy, high-cheeked and handsome,
his head thrown back, his eyes closed,
a well-groomed mustache. Well, it was love,
so to speak, at first sight. I asked John
to speak to him after the service. He was tall,
slender, shabbily dressed but clean
and well-smelling. He wore a snapdragon,
I remember it was yellow and purple,
in his lapel. When our eyes met,
I knew it was mutual. But he looked
at John, and at everyone else
who welcomed him in the doorway,
with the same forever.
We asked him home,
talked with him. Then John,
my dearest John, I'd never known
such pride in him: *Yes you will*
go to college; yes you will
get an education; God
has something big
in store for you; I'll talk
to the president of Simpson College
myself if I have to.
When my eyes met John's
just after he spoke those words,
that was when I knew,
I mean really, really, truly knew,
I meant what I said when I married him.

The Milholland family

The Prayer of Miss Budd

Simpson College, Iowa, 1890

I'd known he was enrolled, but still
the sight of a sepia boy
trembled my foundations,
I must admit. Thanks
for your patience.
They say each teacher
gets one student. Thanks
for giving me mine. Already
I've sent him home three times
with ague: Please watch over him.
When they found out he was living
on prayer and five cents' worth
of beef suet and cornmeal,
so many of our good
Simpson boys gave him
their laundry I'm afraid
for his delicate health.
Keep him warm this winter.
He says he paints to reveal truth,
his colors lucent, almost transparent;
sometimes a square inch of his canvas
is enough to break your heart.
He paints with such lostness
I've had to remind him
that you gave us brushes
because they do some things
better than fingertips.

Father, this semester I've seen
an unequivocal exception
to what has always seemed to me to be
your cockamamie sense of justice.
Now I see the chosen really are
the cornerstones the builders toss aside.
All the battles the Israelites fought
to come home, all that wandering.
The poor women.
And Jesus.

A Negro artist.
Father, give me greater gifts,
so I can teach this master.

Miss Budd's art class, Simpson College. Carver is on the far right.
1890 Carver enrolls at Simpson College, Indianola, Iowa, majoring in art.

The Last Rose of Summer

The paper shakes so
the words are hard to read,
but what good is a singing range
from high D to three octaves below,
what good the bold step to a larger canvas
for the yucca on the easel now,
what good piano lessons paid for
with paintings, what good
a rosebud boutonniere if *Jim*
      your brother
       smallpox

Four a.m. in the Woods

Darkness softens, a thin
tissue of mist between trees.
One by one the day's
uncountable voices come out
like twilight fireflies, like stars.
The perceiving self sits
with his back against rough bark,
casting ten thousand questions into the future.
As shadows take shape, the curtains part
for the length of time it takes to gasp,
and behold, the purpose of his
life dawns on him.

Carver at Iowa State

Cafeteria Food
*Iowa State College of Agriculture
and Mechanic Arts, 1891*

Even when you've been living on
wild mushrooms, hickory nuts,
occasional banquet leftovers sneaked
out of the hotel kitchen by a colored cook,
and weeds; even when you know it feeds you,
mind and body, keeps you going
through the gauntlet
of whispered assault
as you wait in line;
even when it's free
except for the pride
you have to pay by eating
alone in the basement;
even when there's a lot of it,
hot meat or chicken and potatoes
and fresh baked bread and buttery
vegetables; even when there's dessert;
even when you can count on it day after day;
even when it's good,
it's bad.

1891 Carver transfers to Iowa State Agricultural College, Ames, Iowa, believing
that in this way he can better serve the Negro people.

Curve-Breaker
for Mrs. W. A. Liston

What broke the ice?
Was it his G.P.A.? The prayer group
he joined and sustained? The Agricultural
Society he founded, his writing
the class poem and painting the class
picture? His good accent in German Club?
Was it the Art Club? Was it his balancing
an unspilled glass of water on a hoop
to raise funds for new football uniforms?
Was it his soft guitar? His impermeable
arguments in debate? Was it the way
he transformed the cafeteria with vines
and autumn leaves for Welsh Eclectic
Society banquets? Was it his
sidesplitting renditions there
of humorous poems? How the hell
should I know? Maybe it was that white
lady who took the train to Ames to eat
at his table. They both laughed
when she said she was his mother.
Anyway, way before Christmas
we were calling him Doc.

The Nervous System of the Beetle

No, I can top that one. Today
in my Intro to Invertebrates,
we had midterm review.
I asked one of the men
to describe the nervous system
of the beetle. He stood and pronounced,
"The nervous system of a beetle begins
with a number of ganglions
on either side of the thorax
and extends entirely down
on either side of the backbone ..."

What happened? Well,
the class was silent, taking it in.
Then Carver started in to laughing.
He laughed so hard he cried,
until all the others laughed with him,
shaking their heads and exchanging shrugs.
I had to ask him
to explain the joke. By then
the boy who'd said it
had blushed from red to despair
and stumbled from the room.

Carver? He just sat there
wiping tears from his eyes
when I let the class go.

Green-Thumb Boy

Dr. L. H. Pammel

Hybridization, cross-breeding, evolution:
He takes to new theories
like a puppy takes to ice cream.
We whisper that our Green-Thumb Boy
is the black Mendel, that Darwin
would have made good use of Carver's eyes.
So clear his gift for observation:
the best collector I've ever known.
I think we have an entirely new species
of *Pseudocercospora*.
And always in his threadbare lapel
a flower. Even in January.
I've never asked how.

We had doubts
about giving him a class to teach,
but he's done a bang-up job
with the greenhouse. His students
see the light of genius
through the dusky window of his skin.
Just yesterday, that new boy,
what's-his-name, from Arkansas,
tried to raise a ruckus when Carver
put his dinner tray down.
He cleared his throat, stared, rattled
his own tray, scraped his chair legs
in a rush to move away. Carver
ate on in silence. Then the boys

at the table the new boy had moved to
cleared their throats, rattled their trays
and scraped their chair legs as they got up
and moved to Carver's table.

Something about the
man does that, raises the best
in you. I've never asked what.
I guess I'll put his name next to mine
on that article I'm sending out.

Cercospora

Iowa State College, 1895

He smooths a square of butcher paper,
licks his pencil stub, looks up, and loses
himself in the cool of deep woods,
mossy watersong over stones. *This species, with*
conidial scars on the conidiogenous cells ...
Puffballs, *Calvatia gigantea,* curd-white melons
among the leaves. *Boletus edulus* scattered
like gumdrops under the trees: sliced and sautéed
in some sweet butter, with a little bit of chopped onion ...

The door bangs open. White hands,
a blindfold. But he knows that laugh,
and that. But they are white men's
voices, whiteman laughter. But
they are his classmates, his friends.
But they are white men.
White. Pushed and dragged down the street,
into a doorway, hearing the door close behind him,
in whom
does he place his trust?

Standing alone in a hush
of whispers, rustling paper,
in whom can he trust?
He does.
Eyes unbound see,
then do not see
the new suit, shirt, hat, and tie
thrust into his trembling hands.

A Charmed Life

Here breathes a solitary pilgrim sustained by dew
and the kindness of strangers. An astonished Midas
surrounded by exponentially multiplying miracles: my
Yucca and Cactus in the Chicago World Exposition;
friends of the spirit; teachers. Ah, the bleak horizons of joy.
Light every morning dawns through the trees. Surely
this is worth more than one life.

Carver painting "Yucca and Cactus"

1893 Carver's paintings are exhibited at the Chicago World's Fair. *Yucca and Cactus* wins honorable mention for Oil Painting.
1894 Carver gets his B.A. degree.

Called

Tuskegee Institute, 1896

Washington yammers on about his buckets.
Under the poorly pruned catalpa trees
the children of slaves slave on in ignorance.
For what but service is a man thus gifted?
(The set jaw, the toward-distance-looking eyes:
from the fly in the buttermilk, the butterfly in the cave.)
... your salary, duties, the school of agriculture
you will establish, your office key ... A flash
twenty years ahead: this mecca,
this garden. *Good Christ, a whole Africa*
to save, right under my nose.

Carver at Tuskegee

1896 Carver gets his M.A. degree and accepts Booker T. Washington's invitation to
join the faculty of Tuskegee Institute. There he starts a new department and
becomes the first Negro director of a U.S.D.A. Agricultural Experiment Station.

My People

Strutting around here acting all humble,
when everybody knows
he's the only one here
got a master's degree
from a white man's college.
Everybody knows his salary
is double ours. He's got two singles
in Rockefeller Hall; the rest of us
bachelors share doubles. The extra room
is for his "collections."
A pile of you-know-what,
if you ask me.
All that fake politeness, that white accent.
He thinks he's better than us.
Wears those mismatched suits every day, too:
white men's castoffs with the sleeves too short,
the trousers all bagged out at the knees.
His ties look like something
he made himself.
Always some old weed in his lapel,
like he's trying to be dapper.
It makes you want to laugh.
Talking all those big words,
quoting poems at you
in that womanish voice.
So high and mighty,
he must think he's white.
Wandering around through the fields
like a fool, holding classes in the dump.

Always on his high horse, as if his
wasn't the blackest face on the faculty,
as if he wasn't a nigger.

The faculty at Tuskegee. Carver is in the top row, far left.

Odalisque

Listen to this: Now he's asking for
laboratory space and a painting studio!
Says his work *"will be of great
honor to our people."* The
unmedigated gall!
*"I beg of you to give me these,
and suitable ones also."*
Accent on the suitable.
*"I greatly desire to do this that
it may go down in the history
of the race."* Can you believe it,
Mr. Washington?

> At the feet of every listener who hears
> the promise of dawn in the wilderness,
> the peach-luscious, unashamed curves
> of naked ambition.

Chemistry 101

A canvas apron over his street clothes,
Carver leads his chemistry class into
the college dump. The students follow, a claque
of ducklings hatched by hens. Where he
sees a retort, a Bunsen burner,
a mortar, zinc sulfate, they see
a broken bowl, a broken lantern,
a rusty old flatiron, a fruit jar top.
Their tangle of twine, his lace.
He turns, a six-inch length of copper tubing
in one hand. "Now, what can we do with this?"
Two by two, little lights go on.
One by hesitant one, dark hands are raised.
The waters of imagining, their element.

Dawn Walk

The Institute's twenty acres of crops,
its orchards and beehives,
its ten hogs, its dairy herd,
the poultry yard. Landscaping the campus,
testing the wells, overseeing the sewage system.
Directing the first U.S. Agricultural Experiment Station
at a Negro institution, headed by a colored man
(and underfunded).
Chairing the Agricultural Department. Committees:
surely a waste of precious time. Advising.
Students whose toes stick out of their shoes.
Students whose parents were slaves.
Teaching. Their killing ignorance. Heifers
poisoned by dishwater, poisoned by
pruned foliage left on the ground;
bloated ewes scalded to death
by incorrectly mixed dip.
(You'd think they would have stopped
when the first one screamed.)
Their stare of incomprehension.
Our first free generation,
the seeds of our promise.
And only two arms, two hands, two legs,
two eyes, one brain, the time allotted,
and Thee.

From an Alabama Farmer

Dere Dr. Carver, I bin folloring
the things I herd you say last planting time.
I give my cow more corn, less cottonseed
and my creme chirns mo better butter. I'm
riting to you today, Sir, jes to tell
you at I furtulize: 800 pounds
to the acur las March. Come harves, well
it were a bompercrop. How did you found
out you coud use swamp mock? I presheate
your anser Dr. Carver by mail soon.
What maid my cotton grow? It do fele grate
to see the swet off your brow com to bloom.
I want to now what maid my miricle.
Your humbel servint, *(name illegible)*

Laboratory at Tuskegee

Coincidence
15 February 1898

In Wakefield the night train
screeches to a neck-wrenching halt.
Last, the explanation reaches
the Colored compartment,
where Dr. Carver guards in a valise
his jars of Before and After soils
and of compost, his giveaway
bags of raw peanuts.
Hearing down the cars-long voice brigade
a cry for help,
he wonders what in all creation
could make a whole family
sit on the tracks
to try to kill themselves.
He gives thanks
for the engineer's honed eyes.

He looks down at the brown road map
printed in his yellow palms.
Your life may be the only Bible
some people will know.
He rises.

The train arrives only two hours late.

Bedside Reading

for St. Mark's Episcopal, Good Friday 1999

In his careful welter of dried leaves and seeds,
soil samples, quartz pebbles, notes-to-myself, letters,
on Dr. Carver's bedside table
next to his pocket watch,
folded in Aunt Mariah's Bible:
the Bill of Sale.
Seven hundred dollars
for a thirteen-year-old girl named Mary.

He moves it from passage
to favorite passage.
Fifteen cents
for every day she had lived.
Three hundred fifty dollars
for each son.
No charge
for two stillborn daughters
buried out there with the Carvers' child.

This new incandescent light makes
his evening's reading unwaveringly easy,
if he remembers to wipe his spectacles.
He turns to the blossoming story
of Abraham's dumbstruck luck,
of Isaac's pure trust in his father's wisdom.
Seven hundred dollars for all of her future.
He shakes his head.

When the ram bleats from the thicket,
    Isaac ...   like me ...   understands
the only things you can ever
    really ...   trust ...
are ...
        the natural order ...
            ... and the Creator's love ...
    spiraling ...
out of chaos ...

Dr. Carver smooths the page
and closes the book
on his only link with his mother.

He folds the wings of his spectacles
and bows his head for a minute.
Placing the Bible on the table
he forgets again at first, and blows at the light.
Then he lies back dreaming as the bulb cools.

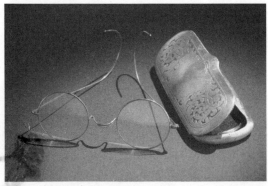

Carver's glasses and case

Poultry Husbandry

Tuskegee, 1902

Raising chickens is a
dawn-to-dawn,
no-Sabbath proposition.
Carver is a botanist.
Yet, bowing before Mr. Washington's mandate,
Carver is named Superintendent of Poultry Operations,
in addition to teaching seven classes,
testing seed, examining soils, running
the Agricultural Experiment Station,
preparing bulletins,
overseeing the dairy's one hundred four cows,
and maintaining a laboratory,
with the assistance of the two or three
work-study students the budget allows.

Washington requires daily
Poultry Yard Reports,
writes from Ithaca
that it doesn't make much sense
to have twenty-seven roosters
for forty-nine hens.
He writes from Syracuse
that there should be twice as many
chicks, given the number of eggs set
and incubated. He writes from Boston
to suggest chicks be purchased.
He telegraphs from New York City
to point out that thirty-nine eggs
are unaccounted for.

Carver answers, "I have faith in the chickens."
But he watches twenty roosters
weed themselves down to ten.
He sees a pecking order established
by ruthless omnivores, by cannibals.
He sees chickens kill each other
out of sheer boredom. He learns
that if you don't stop them,
chickens will peck their pariahs
to ribs and drumsticks.

Slowly, he learns a new vocabulary.
Blackhead: general weakness, unthriftiness,
sulphur-colored droppings. Mortality high.
Sorehead: wart-like nodules covered by black scabs
on bare parts of the head, the feet, and around
the vent. Mortality high.
Coccidiosis: unthriftiness, diarrhea. Mortality high.
Epidemic Tremor: loss of balance,
wobbling gait, prostration, kicking.
Mortality high.
Cholera: Mortality high.
Bronchitis: Mortality high.
Newcastle: Can wipe out
your whole flock.

Toward the end
of one of his daily pre-dawn rambles,

Carver stops at the poultry yard.
He notes the unlocked latch, the gate ajar.
Old Teddy Roosevelt gives the man a beady look,
flaps his wings, stretches
his scrawny, good-for-nothing neck,
and again, hope bleaches the horizon.

Carver working in a lab

1905

Looking out of the front page, a wild-haired,
gentle-eyed young German man stands
before a blackboard of incomprehensible equations.
Meanwhile, back in the quotidian,
Carver takes the school to the poor.

He outfits an open truck
with shelves for his jars
of canned fruit and compost,
bins for his croker sacks of seeds.
He travels roads barely discernible
on the county map,
teaching former field-slaves
how to weave ditch weeds
into pretty table place mats,
how to keep their sweet potatoes from rotting
before winter hunger sets in,
how to make preacher-pleasing
mock fried chicken
without slaughtering a laying hen.
He notes patches of wild chicory
the farmers could collect
to free themselves from their taste
for high-priced imported caffeine.

He and his student assistants bump along
shoulder to shoulder in the high cab,
a braided scale of laughter
trailing above their raised dust.

Today, Carver is explaining,
as far as he understands it,
that fellow Einstein's "Special Theory of Relativity."
He's hardly gotten to Newtonian Space
when a platoon of skinny dogs
announces the next farm.

As they pull up,
a black man and his boy straighten,
two rows of shin-high cotton apart.
With identical gestures they remove
straw hats, wipe their foreheads with their sleeves.
Their welcoming glance meets Carver's eyes
at the velocity of light.

The Jesup wagon

1906 Carver initiates the Jesup wagon, outfitting a horse-drawn wagon to
take his agricultural teaching to the rural poor.

Clay

"Beauty is the vocation
of the earth."—William Bryant Logan

God's breath on a compound of silica,
alumina, and various oxides—
primarily iron—gave Adam life.
There is a primal, almost mystical
connection between humankind and clay,
from the footed, bellied first receptacles
to frescoed Renaissance cathedral walls.
To Carver's eye, the muddy creek banks say
Here, to be dug up, strained, and painted on,
is loveliness the poorest can afford:
azures, ochres ... Scraps of discarded board
are landscapes. Cabins undistinguished brown
bloom like slaves freed to struggle toward self-worth.
Beauty is commonplace, as cheap as dirt.

Carver in the field

Egyptian Blue

From red clay spotted on a hillside
Carver came up with a quadruple-
oxidized pigment the blue
of a royal mummy's innermost windings,
an Egyptian blue
no artist or scientist had duplicated
since the days of old King Tut.
It's the bluest blue,
bluer than lapis.
Paint factories and manufacturers
of artists' materials
begged him for the formula,
offering the top floor of Fort Knox.
He sent it
for the cost of the two-cent stamp
it cost him to mail it.

It's an indescribable blue.
You see it every day
on everything from shutters
to a child-sized flowered dress.
We've learned to live with it
without loving it, as if it were
something ordinary,
that blue the world sought
for five thousand years.
Look around with me: There it is
in the folder on my desk,
in my close-up photo of a fairy tern,

in the thumbtacks in my corkboard
holding up photos, poems, quotes, prayers,
a beaded ancestral goddess juju doll
(it's the blue of the scarab in her hand).
It's the blue of that dictionary
of American Regional English,
of the box of eighty standard envelopes,
the blue of that dress waiting to be ironed,
the blue of sky in that Guatemalan cross,
it's the blue of the Black Madonna's veil.

Paint sample that includes a miniature landscape painted by Carver

The Sweet-Hearts

Sarah Hunt, rumored suicide

Bright as I was,
I knew Mama would suck her teeth
and shake her head with disgust
if she knew we were courting.
He came to the schoolyard
toward the end of every day,
patted the children's heads as they passed,
let them find the roasted peanuts
hidden in his pockets.
Then he would turn to me,
his tawny eyes grow golden.
He'd hand me a flower.

He in his mismatched
secondhand suits
with the top button always buttoned,
always some kind of a flower
in his faded lapel.

He took my books,
offered his arm,
and as we walked
told me about my flower.
Every day a different Latin name.

I flirted.
He talked about the lilies of the field,
about feeding the multitudes with the miracle

of the peanut and the sweet potato.
My invisible, disapproving family.
With him, I could never again ride
in the white car, or sleep in a decent hotel.
He told me of the vision
he'd had on his first day here:
That the school would flourish,
that Tuskegee was the place for him
to be God's instrument.

I straightened his ties,
told him when
his sleeves and collars
needed turning,
suggested he give away
his baggiest trousers,
that there's such a thing
as too much mending.
How he trembled
the first time I took his hand.
That gold light so fierce my shame
was almost burned away.
But our children would be dark,
they might have his hair.
For three years
people smiled at us.
We knew there were whispers:
"The Sweet-Hearts."

He helped my fourth graders
start a garden, talked to them

about growing things.
I wish I'd kept his little notes.
The last one said something like
"Miss Sarah, I believe you care
more about my clothes
than you do about me or my work."
He stopped coming around.
How the children missed him.

I left at the end of the school year
and started a new life. Started you.
Children, you are almost grown,
and I have saved you from Negro shame.
But the man in this clipping
might have been your father.
Charles. —
I can live no longer
this life of a fool.

Dear ones,
forgive me.

c. 1905 Carver meets Miss Sarah Hunt.

A Patriarch's Blessing

1905
Luke 1:68–79

All night the train chug-chugs
toward Missouri. In the last car,
Carver tries to sleep
with his head against the glass.
A few hours later he's showed in,
the thin white face,
white beard to the waist,
and Uncle Mose's right hand
is saying *Come near.*
Carver, his eyes lowered,
kneels beside the rocker.

In Moses Carver's face
the unveiled radiance of Moses' face
when he came down from the mountain.
George, he says. *Carver's George.*
Carver says he's just come back
to get some of those paw-paws
from his favorite tree.
Uncle Mose says if he does,
he's in for a hiding.
Them paw-paws ain't ripe yet.

Moses caresses the stubbly cheek,
cups the bristly chin.
Never could keep you boys away
from my paw-paw tree. Where's my switch?
He pats the soft-crinkled hair
with remembering fingers.
God bless you, my boy.
"For you will go before the Lord
to prepare the way for him."
Unwiped tears
disappear into his beard.

Moses Carver

The Lace-Maker

for P.L.E.

Late Sunday morning gilds the pins and needles,
strokes the wall ochre, blanches the white collar.
He bends, intent on detail, his fingers red
in sunlight, brown in shade. Light calls
through the open to April window directly
into his illumined invisible ear,
like, elsewhere, the trumpet
whisper of an angel.

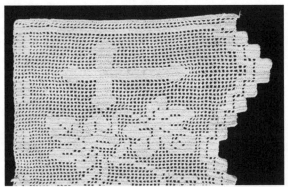

*Carver made time to crochet, knit, and do needlework. He found these activities
satisfying and they enabled him to make useful gifts for his friends.*

Chicken-Talk

1909: So many chickens were missing,
and Washington so hounded Carver's heels,
that Carver bought replacements secretly
and smuggled them into the poultry yard.
In 1910, seven hundred sixty-five
were unaccounted for, and Washington
sent Carver almost daily telegrams
tallying all the missing. Folks in town
said they were "being liberated by ol' John."
They told about how "back in slavery days ..."

> The night was as dark as a barracks
> on Goree Island. John stepped to the doorway,
> and stepped back. Mariah held the baby close,
> her soft palm over his mouth. "He out there?"
> John leaned into the night, his face
> tasting its breezes. He looked back
> and shook his head. He clutched his juju,
> looked at his woman, and clenched his eyes
> in a prayer to the Ancestors. He ran out.

> The gate hinge creaked, but John slipped in
> through an inches-wide gap. No feather stirred
> as he entered the sleeping coop, until
> a stupid biddy squawked warning
> and the flock burst with alarm.
> John stood, shushing.
> "It ain't the fox, fool; it's me, your friend."
> The melee fell to murmuring.

John's fist was under a fat warm hen
when a voice rose in the yard.
"Yes, I did remember to load it. Will you
get on back in the house?
(That damned fox!)"

Uh-oh, John, you in bad trouble.
He gone to get you this time.
You say no?

As Master's boots crunched toward the door,
a faint voice trebled inside.
"Who's in there?"
Master took another step.
He heard the voice again.
Then another, another.
"I say who's in there?"
He cocked his shotgun, stepped again.

Ain't nobody here but us chickens.

Master just went on home,
according to John's children and John's
children's children and their children and theirs. And John
never told on Brer Fox.

The Joy of Sewing

First the threading of the needle,
that eye nearly invisible
held nearer and farther away,
so the tip of the thread
is a camel through a keyhole,
a rich man
carrying all of his belongings
through the Pearly Gates.
But at last, near cussing,
you thread the filament
into the orifice. *Aha!*
The cloth lies on your lap
like an infant in a christening gown,
as smooth under your palm
as your mother's lost skirts.
The needle slow at first,
jackrabbits straight and true.
The making.
The focus.
The stitches your fingers' mantra.

The finished products of contemplation:
the ties Carver always wears
with his secondhand suits.
And the snickers behind his back.

Veil-Raisers

Sometimes one light burned late
in The Oaks, the stately home of the great
Principal, Booker T. He sat and wrote
note after note, controlling faculty,
philanthropists, and family
with spiderweb reins.
When a plank broke and he plunged
into white hopelessness,
he shook himself
and rang up to the third floor,
where a student exchanging service
for tuition sproinged to his feet.

The breathless summons reached
Carver's cluttered rooms
down in Rockefeller Hall,
where he dozed in his easy chair.
He still had lab notes to write,
tomorrow's classes to prepare,
letters, and his Bible reading.
He'd been up, as always,
since that godliest hour
when light is created anew,
and he would wake again
in a few more hours.
Roused, he nodded,
exchanged slippers for brogans.

You saw them sometimes
if you were sneaking in past curfew,
after a tête-à-tête on a town girl's porch:
shoulder to shoulder
and dream to dream,
two veil-raisers.
Walking our people
into history.

Booker T. Washington

The Year of the Sky-Smear

1910

That smear among the stars:
Science may call it Halley's Comet,
but backwoods farm folks say
it's an iceberg headed for a ship's hull,
a chomping mouth trailing its hunger.
They say it's a millennial sign.
The old ones who remember the last
Year of the Sky-Smear,
deep in the birthing throes
of a nation conceived in slavery,
tell of portents they've heard of
since childhood, portents they've seen,
prophecies come true.
They know that history
is a jetsam of stardust.

Back from an afternoon on the road,
elated by the faint glimpse, over dark trees,
of the comet in the twilight,
Carver inhales the homecoming aroma
of his cluttered digs.
He'll have to remember to mail
that parcel to Uncle Mose:
a new pair of long johns.
And those inquiries about soils:
He'll answer them tomorrow.
He turns on the light,
hangs his jacket on his desk chair,

loosens his tie, and sinks in.
He sorts the new mail.

A couple of letters from manufacturers,
a note from Mr. Kellogg in Battle Creek.
A couple of thank-yous. Offers to pay
for answers the Creator gives
him for nothing. A note
from the school treasurer:
Will you please deposit your paychecks
so I can balance the books?
And a letter from Mrs. Goodwin, whose father,
Moses Carver's grandnephew, Thomas,
was a boyhood chum, almost a cousin.
The joy of rattling the pages open. The joy
Oh my God, Uncle Mose has passed.

1910 Moses Carver dies.

The New Rooster

Tuskegee Poultry Yard, 1902–1913

Carver's right hand ached for a week
after he met his new assistant, George
R. Bridgeforth. From then on, the feathers flew.
Or rather, memos flew. Carver had had
a vision of the meaning of his life:
the work he'd be forgotten for, the dream
that would live on. He knew he bore a seed
whose flowers would bear many seeds. Bridgeforth
dreamed of becoming Principal. His work
was excellent, and Washington was torn
between two favorites.
                  Bridgeforth, if he'd been
a rooster, would have been a Leghorn, tall,
meaty, handsomely plumed. And Carver was
some weird, mutant Sicilian Buttercup,
a doily-making lover of flowers.

I wish to say that you perhaps made an error.
A dozen chickens dead of cholera.
I beg to suggest that we quarantine the sick chickens.
Another nine. And disappearing eggs.
I understand that they are laughing at our ignorance.
But five more peanut products! Two today!
Let us be men and face the truth.
The bulletin on cowpeas: twenty-five
taste-tested cowpea recipes, for soup,
coffee, pancakes, pudding, croquettes; advice
on cultivating cowpeas; a simple

lesson on how legumes repay the soil
the nutrients King Cotton takes, and are
an inexpensive protein for the poor.
It seems to me from what I have seen
of the work that it lacks organization.
"Carver's Hybrid": a new high-yield cotton.
One manly order would save
all trouble and hard feeling.
Two broken incubator thermostats.
You must do business like a man.
Chickens and eggs vanished without a trace.
I am here to work as a man,
and I expect to be treated as such.

A ten-year battle over the Poultry Yard.
Carver submits his resignation, stays,
resigns and stays, resigns again but stays.
Washington juggles titles, finally
divides Carver's responsibilities
in two, and separates the men, making
each Head of a Division. Carver gets
a real laboratory. Bridgeforth gets
the Poultry Yard.

>   And the new rooster crows.

1902 George R. Bridgeforth joins the Tuskegee faculty as Carver's assistant.

How a Dream Dies

It was 1915, the year
of trenches and poison gas,
when Booker T. Washington
rushed home from New Haven
to die in his own bed.
For the first days after the funeral
Carver sat and rocked, sat
and rocked. For months
he could not teach,
would not go into the lab.
He sat in his room, he rocked.
His duties were reduced
to supervising the study hall,
where he sat at the front of the room
staring into his hands.

In a vision the first time they met,
Carver had been shown a lifelong partnership.
He paced the campus. He rocked.
He had seen Washington and Carver together
winning back the birthright of the disinherited.
This is how a dream dies.
In the news Europe's tribal feuds
spread to the colonies,
a conflagration of madness.
As if fifty thousand shot and bayoneted men
strewn in an unplowed field
could make right any righter.
As if might

made wrong any less wrong.
All of the dead are of the same nation.

His presence turned laughter down
to whispers. "He acts like he's lost
his best friend." *Uh-uh: He acts*
like he's lost his faith.

Portrait of Carver

1915 Booker T. Washington dies. The monument erected at Tuskegee in
his honor depicts him lifting a veil from the eyes of a male slave who
is rising from a kneeling position.

Out of the Fire

First came the dream.
Washington's daughter-in-law
told Carver in passing she'd dreamed
dear Mr. Washington had said
Carver will carry on for me.
I have faith in him.
Soon after Mrs. Washington's dream
awoke him, Carver is invited to serve
on the Advisory Board of
the National Agricultural Society.
Shortly after that, the British name him
a Fellow of the Royal Society for the Arts.
A Negro. With a growing list of firsts.

The school's administration commends his work
and honors him with a new title: Professor.
And wartime shortages
find him frequently called
by the government to demonstrate
his sweet-potato flour, his ersatz eggs,
his method of dehydrating foods;
or to decipher the composition of
and make visible the enemy's
secret-code inks. At last,
his products and processes

are being used. Discovered
by the war machine.

The Professor is humbled.
He sees how disaster
is seeded with triumph, how
a man is purified by despair.

Carver painting as an old man
1916 Carver is elected a Fellow of the Royal Society for the Arts.

The Wild Garden
c. 1916
Genesis 1:29

The flowers of *Cercis canadensis,*
ovate *Phytolacca decandra* leaves,
the serrate leaves of *Taraxacum officinale,*
Viola species and *Trifolium pratens* flowers,
a handful of tulip petals,
a small chopped onion, a splash of vinegar,
a little salt and pepper and oil, and voilà!
Would you like a second helping?
The Creator makes nothing
for which there is no use.
There are choice wild vegetables
which make fine foods.
Lepidium species, a common dooryard pest,
can be cooked up as greens.
Cirsium vulgare stems,
harvested with gloves and scissors
in a roadside ditch
and stripped of thorns,
can be steamed, drizzled,
and pulled through the teeth
so the delicious heart
oozes to the tongue.
Mmmmmmm ... Oh, excuse me.

If all crops perished, the race could survive
on a balanced diet of wild vegetables.
The homeliest, lowest,

torn out by the roots, poisoned;
the "inferior," the "weeds"—
They grow despite our will to kill them,
despite our ignorance
of what their use might be.
We refuse to thank them,
but they keep on coming back
with the Creator's handwritten invitation.
Another *Hemerocallis* fritter?
Try some of this *Potentilla* tea.

Carver in the field

The Dimensions of the Milky Way

Discovered by Harlow Shapley, 1918

Behind the men's dorm
at dusk on a late May evening,
Carver lowers the paper
and watches the light change.
He tries to see earth
across a distance
of twenty-five thousand light-years,
from the center of the Milky Way:
a grain of pollen, a spore
of galactic dust.
He looks around:
that shagbark, those swallows,
the fireflies, that blasted mosquito:
this beautiful world.
A hundred billion stars
in a roughly spherical flattened disc
with a radius of one hundred light-years.
Imagine that.
He catches a falling star.
Well, Lord, this
infinitesimal speck
could fill the universe with praise.

Ruellia Noctiflora

A colored man come running at me out of the woods
last Sunday morning.
The junior choir was going to be singing
at Primitive Baptist over in Notasulga,
and we were meeting early to practice.
I remember wishing I was barefoot
in the heavy, cool-looking dew.
And suddenly this tall, rawbone wild man
come puffing out of the woods, shouting
Come see! Come see!
Seemed like my mary janes just stuck
to the gravel. Girl, my heart
like to abandon ship!

Then I saw by the long tin cylinder
slung over his shoulder on a leather strap
and his hoboish tweed jacket
and the flower in his lapel
that it was the Professor.
He said, gesturing,
his tan eyes a blazing,
that last night,
walking in the full moon light,
he'd stumbled on
a very rare specimen:
Ruellia noctiflora,
the night-blooming wild petunia.
Said he suddenly sensed a fragrance
and a small white glistening.

It was clearly a petunia:
The yellow future beckoned
from the lip of each tubular flower,
a blaring star of frilly, tongue-like petals.
He'd never seen this species before.
As he tried to place it,
its flowers gaped wider,
catching the moonlight,
suffusing the night with its scent.
All night he watched it
promise silent ecstasy to moths.

If we hurried, I could see it
before it closed to contemplate
becoming seed.
Hand in hand, we entered
the light-spattered morning-dark woods.
Where he pointed was only a white flower
until I saw him seeing it.

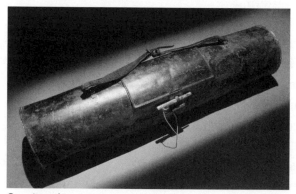

Carver's specimen case

Professor Carver's Bible Class

After Alvin D. Smith

I'd always pictured God as a big old
long-bearded white man throned up in the sky,
watching and keeping score. I had been told
we get harps or pitchfork brimstone when we die.
Superstitiously, I watched for "signs,"
living in fear of a Great Master's wrath.
Professor Carver's class gave me the means
to liberation from that slavish faith.
He taught us that our Creator lives within,
yearning to speak to us through silent prayer;
that all of nature, if we'll just tune in,
is a vast broadcasting system; that the air
carries a current we can plug into:
Your Creator, he said, *is itching to contact you!*

Carver's Bible and pocket watch

1913 At the request of students, Carver offers the first of his fifteen-minute Sunday
evening Bible classes. The classes meet weekly for the next thirty years.

Goliath
for J.B.

Another lynching. Madness grips the South.
A black man's hacked-off penis in his mouth,
his broken body torched. The terrorized
blacks cower, and the whites are satanized.
His students ask, in Carver's Bible class:
Where is God now? What does He want from us?

Professor Carver smiles. "God is right here.
Don't lose contact with Him. Don't yield to fear.
Fear is the root of hate, and hate destroys
the hater. When Saul's army went to war
against the Philistines, the Israelites
lost contact, fearful of Goliath's might.

"When we lose contact, we see only hate,
only injustice, a giant so great
its shadow blocks our sun. But David slew
Goliath with the only things he knew:
the slingshot of intelligence, and one
pebble of truth. And the battle was done.

"We kill Goliath by going about
the business of the universal good
which our Creator wills, obediently
yielding to Him the opportunity
to work wonders through us for all of His children.
That's all. Read 1 Samuel 17:47."

House Ways and Means
Protective tariff for peanuts, 1921

The Chair cedes Mr. Carver ten minutes.

Mr. Chairman, the United Peanut Growers
Association wants me to tell you
about the peanut's possibilities.
I come from Tuskegee, Alabama.
I am engaged in agricultural
research. I've given some attention to
the peanut, and I plan to give much more.
I'm greatly interested in southern crops,
their possibilities. The peanut is
one of the most remarkable I know.
If I may have some space to put things down,
I'd like to show them to you ...
... chocolate-covered peanuts ... peanut milk ...
... a breakfast food. I'm sorry that you can't
taste this, so I will taste it for you. Mmmm.

*John Tilson (R–Connecticut): Do you
want a watermelon to go with that?*

Well, if you want dessert, that comes in well,
but we can get along without dessert.
The recent war has taught us that. Now, these
are dyes that can be made from peanut skins.
This is a quinine substitute. A food
for diabetics, low in starch and sugar ...

1921 Carver appears before the U.S. House of Representatives, Committee
on Ways and Means, in support of a protective tariff on peanuts.

Arachis Hypogaea

Great Creator, why
did you make the peanut?
—GWC

Arachis hypogaea may have been
smuggled to North America by slaves
who hid seeds of survival in their hair.
Despite your nakedness, the chains, the stench,
if white men did not eat you, you might come
to a cruel land where, tended by moonlight
and exhaustion, your seed might grow to be
your children's manna in the wilderness.

Arachis hypogaea, or goober,
an annual preferring warmth and sun,
is an attractive plant, resembling clover.
It bears flowers of two distinct genders:
the staminate, or "male," yellow, pretty,
and the inconspicuous pistillate "female."
When fertilized, the pistillate turns down
and corkscrews six inches into the ground.

Each corkscrew, called a "peg," grows one to four
peanuts in the soil near the mother plant;
each shell two of her shots at infinity.
From the laboratory of a slave emerged
a varied, balanced diet for the poor,
stock foods, ink, paints, cosmetics, medicines ...
Promise and purpose, the Ancestors' dream.
"The Peanut Man," we say, and laugh at him.

Lovingly Sons

Everybody wants a piece of him.
The letters heap,
and there are so many
to pray for.
But his Boys,
Carver's Boys,
pray for him.
Dear Dad,
they write,
Dearest Father.
Misspelled, some
tell of cotton crops, of twelve
laying Plymouth Rocks.
George W. Jones signs his
Your lovingly son.
The Blue Ridge Boys
write of their studies,
their hopes to improve the world.

But some letters
are from Boys he picked
out of lecture hall crowds
in Iowa, Pennsylvania,
Alabama, Tennessee,
or after banquets of tribute
whose fêted guest,
with his cap on his knee,
waited in the hall
to be called to the dais

and proclaimed
Genius, Scientist, Saint.

He pointed them out,
asked them to stay.
They always stayed.

Between them,
a five-minute talk
and a lifelong vow
to pray for each other.

They write
My soul's in communion with yours.
They write *You*
must have been praying for me.
I felt so near
you and Jesus.

The Professor stoops late over his skritching,
squinting through spectacles held together
by a little piece of copper wire.
A smile, dancing radiance,
plays over his face.

Friends in the Klan

1923

Black veterans of WWI experienced
such discrimination in veterans' hospitals
that the Veterans' Administration, to save face,
opened in Tuskegee a brand-new hospital,
for Negroes only. Under white control.
(White nurses, who were legally excused
from touching blacks, stood holding their elbows
and ordering colored maids around, white shoes
tapping impatiently.)
      The Professor joined
the protest. When the first black doctor arrived
to jubilation, the KKK uncoiled
its length and hissed. *If you want to stay alive*
be away Tuesday. Unsigned. But a familiar hand.
The Professor stayed. And he prayed for his friend in the Klan.

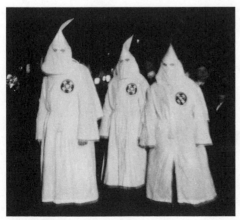

Parade of the KKK

1923 The KKK marches in Tuskegee.
Carver receives the Spingarn Medal for Distinguished Service to
Science, the first of many such honors.

My Dear Spiritual Boy

Letter to Jim Hardwick, October 1923

Your wonderful letter has just arrived.
It is evening; I have some time alone,
so I'm answering right away.
                              My friend, I love
you both for what you are and what you hope
through Christ to be. I am by no means as good
as you believe me. I am sorely tried
so often, and must hide away with God
for strength to overcome. I have suffered
to do the job He's given me in trust
to do. But now He's given you to me
to give me strength, when I needed you most,
confirming my faith in humanity.

A college athlete. White. And a soul mate.
A lonely man smiles at ironic fate.

Carver as an old man

1923 Carver speaks at the Blue Ridge Conference (Y.M.C.A.),
where he meets Jim Hardwick, a student at Virginia
Polytechnic Institute and the first of his "Boys."

"God's Little Workshop"

A hand-lettered sign above
the room number on the closed door.
"Do Not Disturb"
written in the air.
The Professor had had another vision
of an experiment he should try,
a question he should ask.
The Creator's small, still voice
asked *What would happen*
if you made a resin of peanut oil
and added a little bit
of this nitric acid here,
some of that sulphuric acid there,
some alcohol, some camphor,
a little of this, a little of that?
Would the molecules form clusters
tightly bonded into one plastic
which could then be shaped and molded?

A thin, white silence issued
from the door seams,
settled on all who knew
the door was closed again,
made them walk softly,
modulate their laughter,
take themselves seriously.

The Creator asked
What about elasticity?
Is Ficus elastica *the only plant on earth*

whose sap is a latex?
What about Asclepias syriaca?
What about Ipomoea batatas?
Coagulated and stabilized, vulcanized
and compounded with an inert filler,
would their sap become a half-solid, half-liquid
which deforms under applied stress
yet after stretching recovers completely?

The Professor took his Eurekas on grueling
medicine-show lecture tours.
He spoke softly, holding up
his peanut axle grease,
his peanut diesel fuel,
his peanut gasoline,
his peanut insecticide,
his nitroglycerine,
his plastics,
his rubber,
his sleeping compound,
his iron tonic,
his goiter treatment,
his faith, his science,
his miracles.

Eureka
November 1924

His first time in New York,
as one of several speakers
before a conference crowd,
the Professor is allotted twenty minutes.
He abbreviates his talk,
stops abruptly, adds:
I never have to grope for methods;
the method is revealed
the moment I am inspired
to create something new.

The *New York Times* ridicules him,
the school at which he is employed,
and the entire Negro race.
Proving its prophecy, it editorializes:
Talk of that sort simply will bring
ridicule on an admirable institution
and on the race for which it has done
and still is doing so much.
Because REAL scientists
do not ascribe their successes
to "inspiration."

My Beloved Friend
Letter to Jim Hardwick, April 1924

Your letter touched me deeply. How I wish
I was more worthy of the things you say
about me. I love you more dearly because
you are of another race. God is using you
to teach the world the brotherhood of man,
the fatherhood of God. How sweet it is
to let God purge our souls of ego and
bitterness, and to have a little taste
of heaven here on earth. I trust you will pray
for me, that I get rid of my littleness.
I did not have to learn to love you: You
were chosen for me. I knew that the first
time I saw you. It was the Christ in you,
of course.

Driving Dr. Carver

Al Zissler, 1999

Al Zissler's friend Jim Hardwick offered him
a job. It was Spring 1933,
the Great Depression. So Zissler and Jim
drove Carver through the South for several weeks.
At eighty-eight, Zissler recalls picnics:
ham sandwiches, potato chips, sardines
and crackers; Zissler tinkering with the Buick,
Jim reading, Carver gathering salad greens.
They played pranks on each other. Hardwick once
said at a lecture that the Professor was deaf,
and everyone addressed him at the top of their lungs.
But Carver was a genius of mischief:
Later, in his trousers pocket, Jim found a toad.
Falera ha ha they sang along the open road.

*Al Zissler, Carver, and Jim Hardwick combined their spiritual and mechanical energies
to coax an ailing blue Buick along southern highways on a 1933 lecture circuit.*

The Penol Cures
c. 1934

The first wasted child brought to him
for a peanut-oil massage
was carried from the car by his father
and gently laid on a table.
The Professor saw hope
shrink the shadows in their eyes:
Yes, they saw him unalloyed;
they were willing to believe.

He laid on wizened, spidery fingers,
anointing the thin limbs, his eyes closed,
his lips murmuring silence.
After a few weeks of weekly massages
the boy had gained forty pounds
and was chasing pop flies.

Word got out.
The wire services
ran a story about the tentative success
of Carver's Penol treatment for polio.
Crowds arrived at Tuskegee,
children on crutches, in wheelchairs.
Two days a week Carver massaged
as many as his old hands could bear.
Not to mention his seventy-year-old back,
complaining to him all the time
about bending, leaning, pushing,
when all his old heart had to do
was keep pumping its monotonous prayer.

There were many successes,
but many failures as well.
He refused to massage
one red-faced, insistent man
who finally admitted defeat,
turned his chair away,
and cussed out Carver
and his whole misbegotten
sons-of-the-devil race.
There are souls
too crippled to be fixed.

The results of Carver's Penol experiments
were unsatisfactory and irreproducible,
the cause of those cures being
unquantifiable
and wholly unscientific.

Peanut specimen

1933 An Associated Press story about Carver's peanut-oil massages as a
treatment for polio brings throngs of polio victims to Carver's door.

Letter to Mrs. Hardwick

December 1934

My esteemed friend Mrs. Hardwick, I confess
that I have not yet recovered from the shock
of dear Jimmie's marriage. I feel very sure
the dear boy has done well. I did not know
a thing about it! Bless you for writing.
The Professor contemplates his First Boy's joy,
his entrance into a world they will never share.
He signs his shaky name and leans back in his chair.

Carver reading

Baby Carver
Austin Curtis, 1935

Potential assistants strode in
and stumbled out,
repacking their paper credentials.
The Professor, grown more stooped
and now white-haired,
stood a moment beside the door,
then the door slammed.
After all these years of crying out
for another pair of hands
he preferred to work alone,
no young whippersnapper
taking notes over his shoulder.

But young Curtis shook his hand
and disappeared into the student lab.
He resurfaced a couple of weeks later
with six products
from the magnolia seed.
A few weeks later
the Professor wrote to Curtis' father
that Austin seemed to him
more like a son
than an assistant.

Graciously, humbly,
his assistant freed the Professor

from choredom and followed up
on some of his earlier ideas.
Before long Curtis had become
"Baby Carver."
And his children had acquired
a third grandpa.

Curtis and Carver
1935 Austin W. Curtis becomes Carver's assistant.

Mineralogy

for the staff of the Carver National Monument,
Diamond Grove, Missouri

The only thing he still wanted
that a millionaire could buy,
Ford's good friend answered,
was a big diamond.
In Ford's mind,
on Carver's long, skinny, wrinkled
anthracite finger,
a stone to dazzle an entire
classification system of eyes.

Ford told how he bought a flawless
many-carat stone, had it set
in a masculine ring,
and sent it off
gift-wrapped.
When next in Tuskegee
to visit Carver and throw
some money around,
Ford asked where the ring was.
Carver lovingly set aside
several dusty shoeboxes of specimens
and opened a box labeled MINERALS.

He showed Ford his phosphate pebble,
found in an Iowa creek bed,
his microcline feldspar, found
in the Alabama woods, his smoky quartz,

kicked up by his boot toe
in a Kansas wheat field, his fluorite,
sent by a Kentucky spelunker, his
marcasite, sent by an English mineralogist
in exchange for a piece of information,
and here it was, his diamond, the gift
of his dear friend, Henry.

Carver held the ring up to the window.
Ford saw by its faceted luster
that Carver's eyes weren't black, they were brown—
no, they were sparklets of citrine light.

1941 The George Washington Carver Museum at Tuskegee
Institute is dedicated by Henry Ford.

Last Talk with Jim Hardwick

A "found" poem

When I die I will live again.
By nature I am a conserver.
I have found Nature
to be a conserver, too.
Nothing is wasted
or permanently lost
in Nature. Things
change their form,
but they do not cease
to exist. After
I leave this world
I do not believe I am through.
God would be a bigger fool
than even a man
if He did not conserve
the human soul,
which seems to be
the most important thing
He has yet done in the universe.
When you get your grip
on the last rung of the ladder
and look over the wall
as I am now doing,
you don't need their proofs:
You see.
You know
you will not die.

Moton Field

January 1943

From the airfield a few miles down the road
a new droning crowds out laughter from the lawn,
talk in the corridor, automobiles,
and the occasional crow.
There goes one—no, two, three, four:
Like lost geese they circle in practice runs
from sunup to dusk.

The Professor's palsied right hand
stutters answers to letters heaped beside his bed.
Behind them the amaryllis on the sill surrenders
to the cold sky its slow-motion skyrocket.
Beyond the clasped flame of its bud
a P-40 zooms in at five o'clock,
high as a Negro has ever been.

Such a shame, thinks the Professor.
Might-have-been plowshares, hammered
into swords. Sighing, he signs his shaky name
as Nelson tilts the stick to his left, pulls it
slightly toward him, pushes his left rudder pedal,
thumbs-up at the flight instructor, grins,
and makes a sky-roaring victory roll.

1941 The first "Tuskegee Airmen" recruited for an experimental U.S. Army
program arrive at Tuskegee.
1942 On December 9, the fighter pilots of the 99th Air Pursuit Squadron,
the first graduating class of the Tuskegee Airmen, finally receive their
orders to join U.S. combat forces in Europe.

Tuskegee Airman Melvin Moton Nelson (the poet's father) in July of 1944

Commemorative stamp issued in 1948

Commemorative stamp issued in 1998 as part of the "Celebrate the Century" series.

1943 On January 5, in his rooms in Dorothy Hall, George Washington Carver dies in his sleep.

AUTHOR'S ACKNOWLEDGMENTS

First thanks go to Albert J. Price, Captain, Ret., American Airlines, who suggested I write a book about Carver. Thanks to William Jackson, Superintendent, Curtis Gregory, Curator, and Lana Henry, Park Ranger, of the George Washington Carver National Monument in Diamond Grove, Missouri. Thanks to Peter Burchard, whose as-yet-unfinished biography tells the fuller story. Peter, you were so generous with information: Many thanks. Thanks to Mike Jolly, Curator of the George Washington Carver Museum at Tuskegee University, and to Dr. S. H. Settler Jr. of Tuskegee, who shared his memories of working with Professor Carver. Thanks to Dr. Zoran Petrovic of the Kansas Soybean Check-Off Program at Pittsburg (Kansas) State University, for patiently guiding me toward a partial understanding of polymerization and elasticity. Thanks to my cousin, Dr. David Anderson of the University of Louisville, for sending that terrific article about Al Zissler. Thanks to my student assistant, Alyssa Fresa, for helping me with preliminary research. Thanks to Chancellor Mark Emmert and Dean Ross MacKinnon of the University of Connecticut, and to Vanderbilt University, for supporting my research. Many thanks to Benita and Dana Knight for the quiet time at the lake, and to Abba Jacob for quiet time at the hermitage.

And, again, thanks to Pamela Espeland, my editor, my friend.

PUBLISHER'S ACKNOWLEDGMENTS

Special thanks to Cynthia Williams, Chief Archivist at Tuskegee University; to Curtis Gregory and the George Washington Carver National Monument staff; to Al Zissler.

LIST OF POEMS

LIST OF POEMS

PHOTOGRAPHY CREDITS

Tuskegee University Archives

P. H. Polk portrait of Carver, p. 2; George & Jim Carver, p. 12; Carver as a young man, p. 16; Miss Budd's art class, p.23; Carver at Iowa State, p. 25; Carver painting, p. 32; Carver at Tuskegee, p. 33; Laboratory at Tuskegee, p. 39; Carver working in a lab, p. 45; Carver in the field, p. 48; Moses Carver, p. 55; portrait of Carver, p. 67 Carver painting, p. 69; Carver in the field, p. 71; Carver as an old man, p. 82; Carver reading, p. 90; Carver and Curtis, p. 92.

National Park Service, Tuskegee Institute National Historic Site
Photos by Eric Long, Courtesy Museum Management Program, NPS

Slate (TUIN 863), p. 15; spectacles and case (TUIN 1519), p. 42; paint sample (TUIN 285), p. 50; sampler (section) (TUIN 409), p. 56; vasculum (specimen case) (TUIN 1528), p. 74; pocket watch (TUIN 1518) and Bible (TUIN 629), p. 75; peanut specimen (TUIN 1811), p. 89.

George Washington Carver National Monument
The Milholland family, p. 21

Iowa State University
The Faculty at Tuskegee, p. 35

National Archives
Jesup wagon, p. 47

Library of Congress
Booker T. Washington, p. 61; the KKK, p. 81

Al Zissler, Carver, and Jim Hardwick, p. 87, **Al Zissler**
Melvin Moton Nelson, p. 97, **Marilyn Nelson**
Commemorative Carver Stamps, p. 98, **Sanford L. Byrd, ESPER**

NOTES ON FIRST PUBLICATION

"Out of 'Slave's Ransom,'" "Prayer of the Ivory-Handled Knife," "Watkins Laundry and Apothecary" first appeared in *Teacup*. "Drifter" first appeared in *The Poetry Review*. "The Perceiving Self" first appeared in *The New Breadloaf Anthology of Contemporary American Poetry*, edited by Michael Collier and Stanley Plumley (Middlebury College Press, 1999). "Washboard Wizard" and "The Prayer of Miss Budd" first appeared in *Beyond the Frontier*, edited by E. Ethelbert Miller (Black Classics Press, 2000). "Four a.m. in the Woods" first appeared as a broadside published by the Aralia Press (1998). "Cafeteria Food," "Curve-Breaker," "My People," and "Arachis Hypogaea" first appeared in *The Gettysburg Review*. "Green-Thumb Boy," "Cercospora," and "The Nervous System of the Beetle" first appeared in *Gulfcoast*. "A Charmed Life" first appeared in *Literary Cavalcade*. "Odalisque," "Chemistry 101," and "The Lace-Maker" first appeared in *Poetrynet*. "Bedside Reading" and "Coincidence" first appeared in *Spirituality and Health*. "The Wild Garden," "Mineralogy," "Poultry Husbandry," "House Ways and Means," and "'God's Little Workshop'" first appeared in *New Letters*. "Ruellia Noctiflora" first appeared in *The Cortland Review*. "Goliath" first appeared in *The Frost Place Anthology* (Cavankerry Press). "Veil-Raisers" first appeared in *The Emily Dickinson Society Journal*. "Old Settlers' Reunion," "A Ship Without a Rudder," "From an Alabama Farmer," "Clay," "Egyptian Blue," "Professor Carver's Bible Class," and "Friends in the Klan" first appeared in *The Connecticut Review*. The author is grateful to the editors of these publications.